The Secrets and Wonders of Life

Sang Chiong

BALBOA.
PRESS

A DIVISION OF HAY HOUSE

Balboa Press books may be ordered through booksellers or by contacting:

Balboa Press
A Division of Hay House
1663 Liberty Drive
Bloomington, IN 47403
www.balboapress.com.au
1-(877) 407-4847

ISBN: 978-1-4525-0887-0 (sc)
ISBN: 978-1-4525-0888-7 (e)

Printed in the United States of America

Balboa Press rev. date: 1/21/2013

Contents

Chapter 1

The Secrets and Wonders of Life

*E*very human being has a life, yet very few know the truth about life. So what is life? There is only *one* life: the source of all life forms or living things, the *life* of life. It has been called the Tao 道 by Lao Tzu, Heaven by Confucius, God or Father by Jesus, Allah by Mohammed, the Good by Plato, Over-soul by Emerson, and First Cause and Prime Mover by the ancient Greek philosophers.

This life is in you, in me, and in every human being. The life in humans and the life of God are one and the same thing. Both have the same attributes and essence. Both have eternal life, light, wisdom, power, creativity, intelligence, goodness, righteousness, love, freedom, harmony, and peace. A drop of water has the same quality as an ocean of water; the only differences are the volume and size.

Life is a wonder and a miracle, the most precious thing in the universe. The marvel of being alive in the flesh or body is ours only for a few score years on planet Earth. Hence, we must live life to the fullest and enjoy every moment of our existence. The supreme purpose of life is to make a living as well as to make a life, a masterpiece of life.

Human is body and soul, hence the two aspects of life: the material life and the spiritual life. The soul in man is also known as the spirit, self, or mind. It is the soul that gives life to the body. Without the soul, the body is a piece of dead meat, a corpse. The soul is divine and eternal, but the body is material and temporal. Life is body and soul; death is body without the soul. The body is the temporary home and tool of life. Life is more than physical or material but includes the physical body in which life expresses itself. The life that gives life to the body is beyond the five senses—invisible and intangible.

We have only one life and one mind, yet there are two aspects of life with the corresponding two modes of mind: the spiritual, subjective, subconscious mind and the material, objective, conscious mind. The attributes, functions, and workings of the two minds are different and distinct.

spiritual	material
inner	outer
intuitive	intellectual
emotional	rational
synthetic	analytic
artistic	scientific
absolute	relative
involuntary	voluntary

spontaneous	deliberative, habitual
creative	imitative
limitless	limited
natural	artificial
moral	neutral
truthful	factual
idealistic	realistic, practical
imaginative	abstract

The principle of polarity or duality is manifested throughout the universe. Everything comes in pairs and works in pairs: God and matter, yin and yang, cause and effect, stimulus and response, action and reaction, inner and outer, light and darkness, positive and negative, male and female, proton and electron, the binary system, the double helix of DNA, the pair of chromosomes, a pair of wings, a pair of hands, a pair of legs, and so on.

We have two aspects of life with two modes of mind, two hands, two legs, and two lungs to work as one entity. Hence, we must use the pair of legs to walk, the pair of hands to work, the subjective and objective mind to feel and think, and the two aspects of life to live and experience the inner life and the external world of material things. Yin-yang, or polarity, is the working principle of the universe.

As there are two aspects of mind, there are two kinds of knowledge. One entails material, scientific facts from the conscious, objective mind; the other includes spiritual truths from the subconscious, subjective mind. Scientists working with the material, objective mind can only furnish mankind with scientific facts but not spiritual truths. Sages working with the spiritual, subjective mind can inform mankind of their spiritual truths. Facts are objective; truths are subjective. The greatest knowledge, the ultimate truth, is to know Heaven or God. It is the key to all wisdom, understanding, truth, and power.

Both facts and truths are needed for the advancement and betterment of mankind. Progress is continuous improvement and betterment of things and conditions in the external world as well as the innermost world of our lives. Knowledge is power. Only the right knowledge gives us real power.

The purpose of life is to bring out the highest, brightest, and best within ourselves and to enjoy life to the fullest. Excellence in life can only be attained by fully developing and expressing every mode of our existence. There are five modes of existence, and they are the spiritual life, the emotional life, the mental life, the physiological life, and the physical life. Each mode of life is different and distinct in its operation and function, but they are all interrelated and interconnected with one another. They are one and inseparable.

The spiritual life concerns morals, ethics, and values. The soul knows intuitively goodness, righteousness, justice, beauty, peace, harmony, truth, and love. Humans cannot live in a world devoid of goodness and righteousness. We revere Jesus, Confucius, and Gautama because they are good and righteous men. They are men of moral excellence and worthy to be our teachers.

The emotional life is the life of feelings, such as happiness, anger, fear, sorrow, love, hatred, and compassion. Feelings are spontaneous expressions of the soul in response to the external world of things and the inner world of thoughts and sensations. Feeling is the key law and motivating power of life. It is of utmost importance to get our feelings right. Emotional well-being is the absence of depression, anxiety, phobia, worry, rage, hatred, and other built-in ill feelings.

The mental life is the life of thinking and thoughts that includes mindsets, beliefs, theories, doctrines, dogmas, *isms*, suggestions, lies, untruths, facts, and truths. Thought is the most powerful force on Earth. Thoughts can make or unmake us. Thoughts determine what we are. You are what you think. To have a right mind, we must have the right thoughts or truths.

The physiological life is the life of the cells, tissues, organs, systems, and the whole body. The body is a masterpiece. It is made up of trillions of cells, and each cell is so enormously complex that we still do not have a complete understanding of its operation. There are over 100,000 genes and 3.2 billion pairs of biochemical letters in a human cell. It's mind-boggling.

The physical life is the life of action—making and doing. Humans are specially designed by Heaven to stand upright in order to free the pair of miraculous hands. The pair of hands is a wonder itself. It is a master-piece of creation. Our hands are so nimble, so flexible, so versatile that they can perform all kinds of work. Using tools and machines, the pair of hands creates all the wonders of the world: skyscrapers, pyramids, bridges, the Great Wall, the Forbidden City, dams, airplane jets, ocean cruisers, mobile phones, computers, out-rigs, space shuttles, rockets, and countless other creations.

Chapter 2

The Life of Love

God is love, and this divine feeling is inherent in every human being. Love is the secret of life. The light of life is fed by the power of love. Where love is, God is. Love is the highest, greatest, and noblest of all human feelings. To love is to be divine. Love brings out the divinity in Jesus, Gautama, Confucius, and all good men and women who loved their fellow humans. Love is life itself expressed.

Self-love, or the love of oneself, and life are the foundations for all kinds of love: romantic love, maternal love, paternal love, fraternal love, love for humanity, and love of God. If we do not have love in our hearts and souls, we cannot love others. We cannot give what we do not have. We must give love in order to receive love.

From self-love, we can give love to our parents, our children, our friends, our fellow humans, and God. Love gives you joy and pleasure. Love everything that happens to you;

love the things you do; love the life you live; love the house you live in; love nature and God's creation. Love goodness, righteousness, peace, harmony, and all things beautiful.

Love is the greatest unifying power in the world. Love brings all kinds of people together in peace and harmony. Love unites the lover and beloved in marriage. Love unites brothers, sisters, uncles, aunties, fathers, and mothers together in a family. Love brings peace, harmony, and joy to the people.

Love is the absence of hatred, and hatred is the absence of love. Love and hatred are diametrically opposed to one another and mutually exclusive. Where there is love in our soul, there is no hatred in us. Where there is hatred in our hearts, there is no love within us.

> Love makes us divine; hatred makes us satanic.
> Love makes us good; hatred makes us evil.
> Love makes us beautiful; hatred makes us ugly.
> Love brings harmony; hatred brings disorder.
> Love brings peace; hatred brings wars and conflicts.
> Love brings blessing; hatred brings suffering.
> Love brings joy and happiness; hatred brings pain and sorrow.
> Love builds; hatred destroys.
> Love unites; hatred divides and splits.
> Love vitalizes; hatred devitalizes.

Love creates; hatred destroys. It is God's love that creates all things in the universe. God wants love and service for Its creation. There is no better way to love and serve God except toward God's creation. To love and serve our fellow humans, to love and protect the world's environment, to love and protect wildlife and nature, is to love and serve Heaven.

True love is wise and selective, not mechanical and blind. Humans have the wisdom and freedom to love what is good and to withhold love from the bad and the evil. Love cannot be compelled or forced. We have the freedom to choose, to love, or not to love something or someone. We cannot love evildoers, wrongdoers, injustice, cruelty, and ugliness.

Love is mutual, not one-sided. It is to love and to be loved. We love God, and God loves us in return. We love our family, and our family returns the love. We must give love in order to receive. Love and to be loved form a double blessing. It is a blessing to give love to the beloved; it is also a blessing to receive love from the beloved. Love begets love.

Love is active, not passive. To love is to care for the one you bring to this world. A mother's love is manifested as she cares for the well-being of her child. She provides her child with all her needs. She protects her child from harm. She loves, cares, provides, protects, and nurtures her child until he is independent. Loving and caring are love in action.

Where there is love, there is compassion. We cannot bear to see the pain and suffering of our fellow humans. We condemn cruelty and inhumanity towards animals and humans. We help the sick, the poor, the disabled, and the injured. We help the whales that are stranded on the beach. We help our fellow humans in an earth-quake, a storm, a tsunami or any natural disasters. We feel pity when school children are massacred by automatic assault rifles.

Love is divine, the highway to Heaven. Take out love from your life, and you are forever separated from God. Love is essential to our physical and spiritual well-being. Love is vitalizing, invigorating, and energizing, building and creating health. Hatred is the greatest obstacle to health and success. It poisons our blood, tears down the nervous system, and adversely affects all the vital process of the body. Hatred is evil, destroys health, wrecks happiness, and breeds trouble, misfortune, disaster, accident, malice, and resentment. Hatred separates you from God *forever*.

Chapter 3

The Life of Truthfulness

"Absolute Truthfulness is the way of Heaven."
至诚天之道

Chung Yung 中庸

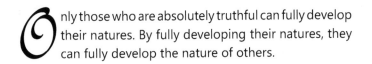

nly those who are absolutely truthful can fully develop their natures. By fully developing their natures, they can fully develop the nature of others.

As there is truthfulness, there will be expression.
As it is expressed, it will become manifest.
As it becomes manifest, it will be full of light.
As it is full of light, it will move others.
As it moves others, it will change them.
As it changes them, they are transformed.
Only those who are absolutely truthful can transform them.

Truthfulness is the end and beginning of things. Without truthfulness, there would be nothing. Therefore the good and the righteous value truthfulness above everything, according to Chung Yung. There is no God higher than the truth.

Without truthfulness, a man is but a hollow mask and whatsoever work he attempts to do, it will be lifeless. Out of an empty vessel, nothing but the sound of hollowness can come; and from insincerity or untruthfulness, nothing but empty words can proceed. By being truthful, we align ourselves with God and the spiritual flow of life. With absolute truthfulness, we radiate light for all to follow.

Truthfulness is the absence of hypocrisy, deceit, deception, fraud, falsity, lie, dishonesty, cheating, pretence, artificiality, misrepresentation, disinformation, presumption, half-truth, and insincerity. For insincerity, even if not seen, is felt, and those who are incapable of giving trust and truth cannot receive it. To be truthful in mind, you must be free from self-deception—you must hate vice as you would a stinking odour and love virtue as you would a thing of beauty.

It is truthfulness that places a crown upon your life above the common people. Your words are direct and powerful because they are true. What is true is a truth; what is false is a lie or untruth. What is right is a truth; what is wrong is untruth.

God is truth. A lie is something that is not. God cannot create something that is not: a lie. Hence, God is truth. All truth or right thought originates and is of God. Whatever is, is right. Truth is the foundation and aim of knowledge and goodness is the foundation and objective of action. We can only understand things by the light of truth. Truth is the awareness of what actually is true and real. Divine Truth is one and eternal; material facts about nature are many and changing. Truth is absolute and eternal whereas scientific facts are relative and changing in relationship with time, space and change.

When you are thinking right about a thing, you are knowing the truth about it. The moment you change your thought about a thing and place it in the right, you are at that moment knowing the truth of that thing. Truth is always right. Truth cannot be wrong. Hence, truth is right thought.

> Truth is the understanding of the mind of that
>   which is true and right.
> Truth is precise verity and reality.
> Truth cannot be added or subtracted.
> Truth is infallible and immutable.
> Truth operates without error.
> Truth liberates, while untruth enslaves.

Truth does not change. If a thing is true today, it will be true tomorrow. If it is true in the beginning, it is true in the end. It is the unchangeable amid the changeable. Truth is good for eternity. Truth is absolute.

Chapter 4

The Life of Goodness

*A*bsolute goodness is the law of God, the way of Heaven. God cannot be partly good and partly evil; the divine is wholly, completely, and absolutely good. God and good, godliness and goodness, godly and goodly: they are one and inseparable. Where God is, goodness is; where goodness is, God is. Goodness is the supreme attribute of God. To be good is to be God.

Moral excellence or absolute goodness is the shortest and most direct way to Heaven. Goodness is inherent in every human being; hence, no human is born evil or with sin. Goodness is the absence of evil or sin; evil or sin is the absence of goodness. Good and evil, they are diametrically opposed to one another and mutually exclusive.

The innermost nature or life is good because it is divine—the exact image of God. Mencius 孟子 the second sage after Confucius 孔子 affirmed the goodness of human nature.

To know one's nature is to know Heaven. Human is the individualized life of God, and Heaven is the universal life.

The most important word in the teaching of Confucius is *ren* 仁 or goodness. It is the supreme virtue, the highest of all virtues, the foundation or moral philosophy, the way of the sage. We know nothing higher than goodness. We can conceive of nothing more perfect than goodness, nothing more beautiful than goodness. Where there is goodness in the soul, there are love, compassion, righteousness, justice, peace, and harmony; it is the complete absence of evil, hatred, disharmony, wrongdoings, and evildoings.

Goodness is a fundamental ethical value. It is indefinable and cannot be analysed. Goodness is a divine attribute upon which all ethics depends. Human civilization cannot function without goodness. How is goodness to be defined? Simply by the child's definition that what is bad is not good and what is good is not bad. We all know what is good and what is not good intuitively. A good man, wishing to establish his own character, also establish the goodness of character in others, and wishing to be successful himself, also help others to be successful. Only those with goodness know what goodness is, such as Jesus, Gautama and Confucius.

The supreme learning (*ta hsueh*) 大学 is to bring out the brilliant virtue, to love the people, to attain the highest good or absolute goodness. The first lesson in life is to learn that all good comes from Heaven, the only source and foundation of good. For Confucius, goodness is the true essence of what it means to be the best human. Although goodness is an inborn quality, the manifestation of it is rare indeed. Only a few sages can manifest the goodness within.

To Plato, God is the Good. "Good" is the closest synonym and the adjective used to describe God.

God is totally and absolutely good and this divine principle within us means that we always seek what is good or do what is good. The God within us is always moving toward goodness. It is an absolute essence which lights the intelligible world, the guide for all right actions.

Goodness brings peace, harmony, justice, love, creativity, prosperity, well-being, righteousness, and happiness to the individual and the nation. Evil brings destruction, war, disorder, injustice, hatred, poverty, corruption, pain, and suffering to the people. Goodness is the foundation of right actions and truth is the foundation of all knowledge.

Chapter 5

The Life of Rightness

Goodness 仁 (ren) is the inner essence of being, and rightness 义 (yi) is the outer manifestation of goodness. 仁义 Ren yi, goodness and righteousness, are two words that always go together; they are one and inseparable. They are goodness within, rightness—doing the right thing without. The way of Heaven can be summed up in one sentence: whatever is, is right. The law of righteousness is the absolute law that rules supreme in the universe and human civilization. Doing the right thing is the law of God, the law of life, and the law of humanity.

Rightness and goodness are simple and unanalyzable properties; they cannot be explained in terms of feelings, nor are they scientifically discoverable according to William David Ross. The property of rightness, he says, is simple and nonanalyzable, and the concept of "right" is indefinable. Our conscience know what is right or wrong. It is an unmistaken feeling that informs us not to do something wrong or evil.

If we proceed with the wrong doing, we will feel guilt and remorse for the rest of our life, whenever we bring it into awareness.

Goodness and rightness (ren yi) is the foundation of human civilization. Doing the right thing will rid the world of all wrongdoings and crimes, such as murder, rape, robbery, fraud, exploitation, injustice, slavery, inhumanity, racism, violence, and every kind of evildoing. Always do the right thing, and everything will be right in life, in the family, and in the nation. Right doing is the absence of all wrongdoings and doing the wrong thing.

Human lives are built on the unshakable foundation of what is absolutely right and true. They cannot be built on the basis of errors, mistakes, and lies. To have a right mind, we must have the right thoughts or truths. Wrong thoughts, lies, and untruths will not make a right mind.

When the mind is right, we can think right, feel right, do right, and live right. With a right mind, we can do the right thing in the right way, in the right place, and in the right time. When the mind is not right or sick, then everything is wrong—wrong thinking, wrong feelings, wrongdoings, and wrong living. We have only one life on planet Earth. Can we afford not to get it right? All the wrongs in the world come from wrong thoughts, wrong feelings, and wrongdoings.

Right thoughts are truths; wrong thoughts are untruths or lies. To have a right mind, we must rid our minds all wrong thoughts, wrong beliefs, wrong theories, wrong knowledge, wrong information, and everything that is not right. Is the theory of evolution right? If not, we must get rid of it. Is the theory of creation right? Always seek the truths. Know the truth, and the truth will set you free. Free from what. Free from ignorance, stupidity, poverty, sickness, bondage, errors, and all kinds of evils.

The right mind is the enlightened mind, one with the light of God. A right mind has only right thoughts or truths. Never clutter your mind with trash, nonsense, triviality, beliefs, and all kinds of useless knowledge. Do a thorough mental house cleaning and get rid of all the useless junk. Truth is the foundation and aim of knowledge and is a prerequisite to an enlightened mind.

Wisdom is the power to perceive the best ends to aim at and the best means for reaching those ends. It is the power to perceive the right thing to do. Only God, who is absolutely good and wise, knows the right thing to do at all times. Whatever is, is right. Wisdom is dependent on the right knowledge and right thoughts. Wisdom is to know God, the source of everything in the universe: goodness, truth, creativity, and harmony.

Chapter 6

The Life of Beauty

*T*he Infinite Goodness behind all natural phenomena is a God of beauty. Beauty is an attribute of God. A thing of beauty is a joy forever. We are surrounded by beauty: beautiful flowers, colourful birds, pretty fishes, lovely men and women, lovely sunrises and sunsets, and majestic nature. Nature is art designed by the Greatest Artist for all to admire and appreciate. Beauty is a joyful experience in appreciating the wonders and creativity of God's universe. Because we are divine essence of beauty, we appreciate it in the natural world.

The path of beauty leads to Heaven or God. All that is truly beautiful is so because it is the impression of the God of beauty. When we admire and appreciate beauty, we are admiring and appreciating the Creator of beauty. A lover of beauty is a lover of God's wonderful creation. If you forget beauty, you forget God. Love of beauty brings us in touch with Heaven, one with the Creator of beauty. God is also known as the good, the true, and the beautiful.

If beauty and a deep love of beauty are not part of your life, then your soul is not awakened or enlightened. If your soul lacks beauty, there is no beauty in your life. There is no greater evil than the perpetuation of ugliness for mankind. Ugly environment creates sickness and unhappiness within the soul of man and ultimately affects our health and well-being.

When beauty is a permanent part of our life, we cannot tolerate any form of ugliness, such trash, rubbish, junk, pollution, impurity, untidiness, filth, imperfection, flaw, blemish, fault, disorder, disharmony, wrongness, vandalism, the indiscriminate destruction of God's creation.

What is the best education? Plato had the right and best answer: "It is that which gives to the body and the soul all the beauty and all the perfection of which they are capable." The life that would be complete, that would be sweet and sane as well as strong, must be softened and enriched by a love of the beautiful. "Beauty is God's Handwriting," said Emerson.

Let us make the world a better place by putting more beauty not for ourselves but for all humans and their future generations. Let us protect God's creation and the natural environment from pollution, defilement, and destruction. Let us protect the lovely animals and flowers from extinction. Vandalism and indiscriminate destruction are acts against humanity and God.

Beautiful flowers are silent messengers from God. When we truly admire and appreciate the lovely design and creation of the flower, we get in touch with the Infinite Beauty, which gives them birth. Cut off beauty in your life, and you cut off God completely. When you are in touch with beauty, you are in touch with God. The more we see beauty in a child, in a woman, in the external world, and in the inner world of ourselves, the more we see God.

A lovely smile of a beautiful, good woman reveals a lovely soul within. It is the outward manifestation of the innermost beauty. A beautiful smile is something which remains in our memory, an unforgettable experience, like the lovely smile of Mona Lisa in the painting. No one can resist a lovely smile or a hearty laughter. It is so inspiring, electrifying, powerful, and life lifting. Beauty awakens the love of life. It helps to perpetuate life on earth. Beauty creates love and love perpetuates life. We love what is beautiful, true and good. Love makes us divine and one with God.

Surround yourself with beautiful songs and music, beautiful pictures and objects, lovely flowers, beautiful dresses, and all things beautiful. When we are tired or discouraged, let us find inspiration and joy in a beautiful flower, in a lovely song or music, in the beauty and wonders of nature. Without beauty, life will be like a desert: barren and lifeless. Devoid of beauty, your nature will be hard, cold, joyless, and unattractive. Now is the time to put beauty into our lives—a little every day. Everything grows from small to great until we are inseparable from beauty and one with beauty and God.

Beauty gives us joy, pleasure, peace, harmony, love, zest, and enthusiasm in life. The love of beauty plays a very important role in our poised, balanced, and well-proportioned life.

Beauty is a great refresher, health promoter, and life giver. It is a magical, miraculous, and wonderful gift from God to enrich our lives. Beauty is related to accuracy, balance, creativity, coherence, contrast, consistency, goodness, harmony, proportion, symmetry, colours, order, originality, love, expression, truthfulness, and many others.

The Infinite Beauty is also a God of goodness, rightness, truth, power, intelligence, wisdom, creativity, love, light, excellence, perfection, freedom, and life.

Chapter 7

The Life of Power

God is Almighty Power, the source of all powers in the universe: atomic power, electrical power, magnetic power, and solar power. Power is the ability to create things, to do things, to move things, to attract or repel things, to change things, to materialize or dematerialize things. To create is to generate, design, produce, make, materialize, form, empower, and grow all things. It is also a forming power that gives forms and shapes to all living and non-living things. The Tao does everything through *wu-wei*, 无为 or effortless action.

The power in human is the same as in the Almighty Power. This power is called life power or life force, and in Chinese, it is *qi* 气. It is the life power that gives life to the body. It is the power that gives movement to the hands and legs as well as the heart and lungs. This power must be recharged every night during sleep.

Throughout all nature, there is a miraculous power at work moving the planets around the sun; it is an orderly solar system with perfect harmony between its parts. Order and harmony constitute God's first law. The Earth rotates and revolves in an orderly orbit without fail year after year. There is no chaos or disorder in the solar system and in the universe. As a norm, everything is in order and operates harmoniously, but there can be sudden and unexpected changes in the weather or climate.

Man, like God, has the power to create via his thoughts and feelings. Every created thing, including the pyramids, Great Wall, airplane jets, automobiles, computers, and nuclear power stations, must begin as a thought or picture in the mind of man. The power to think and visualize is the starting point for all man-made things. Mental creation must come first before the physical creation. If it is not in the mind, it is not in the world.

Humankind has used solar power, nuclear power, electrical power, and magnetic power to improve their lives. They can also employ the Almighty Power for the betterment of mankind. It is an intelligent power, not blind forces, and is forever responsive to our good intentions to improve the lives of the human race. The purpose of life is growth, development, improvement, betterment, and continuous progress.

Chapter 8

The Life of Faith

*F*aith creates success. To him that believes, all things are possible. It is faith that everywhere does the impossible. It is the faith in God and faith in oneself, a divine self-confidence that make men gods whose will must be obeyed. Self-confidence is a prerequisite to success, a real creative force to make things happen.

Faith has been the miracle worker of the ages, a connecting link between human and God. Faith is the absence of doubt, fear, uncertainty, insecurity, confusion, negation, and failure. There is no philosophy or power in the universe that can help you to do a thing when you think you can't do it. If you think you can't, there is no way you can do it, attain it, or make it a success. Lack of faith or self-confidence is the major cause of failure. No one can achieve anything worthwhile when his power is paralyzed by doubt, which makes a certainty of failure.

Men who have succeeded in the world have been firm believers in their destiny. The world makes way for the man who believes he was born to play a great part in the lives of humankind. Nothing could shake, and nothing could stand in the way of, a man of destiny who believes in his mission and his resolve to make it a success.

A human who believes in his destiny, who has the unquestioned faith his mission, who believes he is doing God's work, who believes he is serving humanity and making the world a better place, will succeed. People will follow those who have the faith in their destiny or mission to change their lives for the better. All great men and history makers had an unshakable conviction in regard to their work or mission.

According to your faith, it is done unto you. To succeed in life, you must have complete confidence in yourself, faith in the Almighty to give you a helping hand, faith in your fellow humans, and everything to help you. Faith gives us courage, zest, enthusiasm, hope, persistence, determination, power, and will to make it a success. Without faith, we can do nothing, and we will fail.

Chapter 9

The Life of Happiness

*E*very human seeks happiness. Can we seek happiness the same way we seek wealth or money? Those who seek happiness will not find it. What is happiness? Happiness is a feeling. A feeling of happiness cannot arise by itself. It is aroused by something inside and outside us. There are many things that make us happy, and there are many things that make us unhappy. Seek the things that make us happy and avoid those that make us sad. It's as simple as that.

Know God. God is the source of all happiness, bliss, and blessing. When you are one with Heaven, you have an eternal companion and protector. Our first priority in life is to know God. Mencius said, "To know one's nature is to know Heaven." Alexander Pope advised, "Know then thyself, presume not God to scan."

Be self-sufficient. When you do not depend on others for a living and have the resources to take care all your basic needs, you feel content and happy. You cannot be happy if you do not have a roof over your head, a job, or money to buy the things to sustain your life.

Be healthy. Health and well-being give us happiness. You cannot be happy if you are sick and unwell. You worry about your health and spend a fortune to get well. No one can be happy if he or she is sick and in pain; the person will have only sorrow and suffering.

Be free. Be your own master, and live your own life. Have the freedom to do what you like. If you are dependent on others and cannot live your own life, you cannot be happy. When you are free, you are not sad. You are content with life.

Be yourself. To discover your unique, free self is the greatest joy in life. You discard the mask and the personality you acquired when you were young. You are no longer an impersonator but your true self.

Be loving. Love yourself, love God, and love your family and friends. To love and care for your fellow humans, give you joy and happiness. Love nature and its wildlife. Love and enjoy the beauty around you.

Do good deeds. If you give to the world the best that you have, the best will come to you. The deepest and highest joy is to render valuable service to mankind by giving inspiration, hope, a better future, and a better world.

Doing the right thing gives you joy and happiness. Wrong doing or doing the wrong thing can never give you peace of mind and happiness. Wrong doing pricks our conscience and generate ill feeling of guilt or remorse. People with remorse can never be happy. Happiness is the absence of ill feelings such as guilt, remorse, envy, hatred, rage, grief and anger. When feelings are not aroused, we are in a state of perfect equilibrium or peace.

Help and serve your fellow humans are the surest way to make you happy. Those who helped the injured victims from earth-quakes, storms, tsunamis and other natural disasters had a deep soul joy for rendering valuable service. To save lives is the highest of all services.

Be creative. To create something new and useful for the service of mankind is a joy forever. The whole world is grateful for the wonderful inventions such as electricity, cars, computers and thousands of useful tools and machines. Learn new things, learn to play a musical instrument, to cook a new dish. It gives you happiness to create a new dish, cook it and enjoy the food. Success in everything we create and do gives us the greatest happiness.

Enjoy the simple things in life. Enjoy beautiful songs and music. Enjoy the food you eat. Enjoy the beauty of nature. Be happy that you are alive and well. Be happy with what you have, what you do and what you are.

Chapter 10

The Life of the Self

*Y*ou have only one self, yet there are two aspects of self that were made known to the whole world by R. L. Stevenson in his work *The Strange Case of Dr. Jekyll and Mr. Hyde.* One is the original true self, your unique individuality; the other is the acquired artificial self, your personality.

Personality comes from the word *persona*, meaning "a mask." A personality is someone wearing a mask and impersonating someone. He is someone who assumes a false appearance or a false identity and is an actor or impersonator.

"God has given you one face and you make yourself another," Shakespeare said. God has given you a face, your individuality, and you make yourself a mask, a personality.

Your acquired self or artificial personality is the sum total of your habits, mindsets, conditioned feelings, unchanging beliefs, mechanical actions, same old self, same old lifestyles, addiction to drugs, religious indoctrination, training, and upbringing.

In all this world, there is not another you, nor has there ever been another you. It is silly to mould yourself into a likeness of your fellows, to undo the work that God has done. You are born here on Earth in the form that is different and unique among your billion fellow humans. You can only live the life that is uniquely yours. God produced no other person like you. Only you can be you. Your purpose in life is to be yourself and more of yourself.

Be yourself, your very best self, your very greatest self, and your character will be developed. A God-like individuality within will manifest a good and righteous character without. Your divine self knows intuitively what is good or evil, right or wrong. The artificial personality follows blindly the standard of public opinion of prescribed goodness and rightness.

To be your true self is to be the master of your whole life: to live your own life, to think your own thoughts, to express your real feelings, and to do your own thing. This is true freedom, the birthright of every human. You are the master of your own destiny and future.

The secret of all secrets is to know the truth concerning the true self. The true self is the individualized God within your body. The God inside you is the same as the God outside you. One is finite; the other is infinite.

The true self or the God within is timeless and eternal, without beginning or end. It is eternal life. Without the divine life within, the body is lifeless. Your true self is a giant self dwarfing into nothingness your petty self or artificial personality.

The divine self knows what is good or evil, right or wrong. It does not err. It knows intuitively without learning or reasoning. Reason cannot differentiate absolutely between good and evil or right and wrong, and we can be misled by rationality. The most learned professors can reason wrongly and make mistakes in their judgments and conclusions.

"This above all: to thine own self be true."

Shakespeare

"Know then thyself, presume not God to scan, the proper study of mankind is man."

Alexander Pope

Chapter 11

The Life of Habits

Habit is not only second nature, it is ten times nature. Practically all our daily behaviours and actions are habits. The way we walk, the way we talk, the way we eat, and the way we work are effortless actions of automatism. We are creatures of habits—mere robots and automatons.

There are hundreds of habits: drinking, smoking, eating, swearing, walking, driving, etc. There are good habits and bad habits, right habits and wrong habits, useful habits and useless habits. Habits are fixed, unchanging behaviours or actions.

A habit is formed through continuous repetitions. When we do a certain thing day in and day out over a long period of time, it becomes a habit. Once formed, it is very difficult to break a habit. The most important thing in life is to form good, useful habits and break bad, useless habits. Make habits our friend and not our enemy.

It is good that all our daily activities are effortless actions of automatism. Life is miserable if we have to think and deliberate on every simple act of drinking, eating, and sleeping. Habits save time and effort. Be a master of your habits, not a slave.

We are aware of our physical habits, but we are unaware of our mental habits. Every human has mindsets. A mindset is a doctrine, theory, belief, or any other thought that is deeply set or rooted in the subconscious, subjective mind and accepted as truth. A mindset is fixed and unchanging. It is almost impossible to change the mindset of another person.

Mindsets set the mind for life. We have a closed mind, no longer open to new ideas or thoughts. We reject any ideas or thoughts that do not conform to our mindsets. Fixed beliefs close the mind to new ideas. Mindsets or paradigms determine the way we think and the way we live our lifestyles. They determine how we look at life, abortion, religion, politics, people, conservation, global warming, and relationships.

People are different because their mindsets are different. What the world is today is the manifestation of our mindsets. To change an individual, a nation, or the world, we must first change the mindsets. The future and destiny of the world depend on our changing wrong habits and wrong mindsets.

Chapter 12

The Life of Success

*G*etting what you want is success; attaining what you desire is success; winning is success. Not getting, not attaining, and losing are failure. Success is synonymous with achievement, accomplishment, attainment, creation, production, possession, fulfilment, completion, improvement, advancement, development, prosperity, wealth, and results.

Success is an effect or result coming from the employment of a cause. Success is essentially the same in all fields of human endeavour. The difference is in the things the people desire. Success results in the attainment of a particular desire, whether it is wealth, health, happiness, peace, harmony, fame, power, or position. Success is attaining without regard to the thing attained.

The cause of success is always in the individual. It is some power within that individual that is the cause of success.

Know what the cause of success is and how it can be used to make something a success. To succeed, you must have the unshakable faith that you can succeed.

There are scores of desires, hence numerous ways to attain them. Attaining health is different from attaining wealth. The ways and means of attaining them are different. To succeed, we must use the right way and the best means to attain what we want.

True success is based on service. It is only by our service to mankind that we can ever find happiness, and this is, in itself, true success. To serve mankind brings the truest and most lasting success. One who finds one's success in service and in making the world a better place for future generations is most truly successful. The more good a person can do for humanity with his product, his service, his life, or whatever it may be, the greater the success that person will have. Give the world your best, and the best will come back to you. That is everlasting success.

The greatest success in life is to bring out the brightest, the highest, and the best within oneself and to be a partner with Heaven for the betterment of mankind. Thinking, feeling, and doing are the keys to all success. Thoughts and feelings are the origin of all things, and one's thoughts and feelings are the same as Heaven. Action plus thought and feeling will make every desire a success.

Chapter 13

The Life of Feelings

When feelings of joy, anger, and sorrow are not aroused, it is called perfect equilibrium; when feelings are aroused and expressed rightly and hit the mark, it is called harmony, according to Chung Yung.

Feelings are essential to life. Without feelings, life is not worth living. Feeling is the law of life; it is life itself. Devoid of feelings, a human is a thinking machine or mere automaton that is cold, mechanical, and unlovable. Feeling is the motivating force in life, and we act according to our like and dislikes.

Feelings of fear, joy, and anger are spontaneous expressions of the soul in response to the external world of things and the internal world of thoughts and sensations. Feelings inform us of the true nature of the situation. Natural spontaneous feeling does not err. It is always right.

The external world of things, people, nature, events, conditions, situations, circumstances, happenings, and news generates appropriate or right feelings. The internal world creates thought, sensation, dream, nightmare, and imagination aroused feelings naturally and spontaneously. In a nightmare you woke up shaking with fear. Your natural, spontaneous feelings are always right in response to the real situation: they cannot be wrong. Always trust your first natural, spontaneous feeling.

There are many kinds of feelings. They are fear, happiness, anger, sorrow, hatred, likes and dislikes, compassion, pity, jealousy, love, envy, anxiety, depression, and worry. Feelings can be good, positive, and creative; they can be bad, negative, and destructive.

Feelings must be expressed, not suppressed or repressed. Feel happy when the occasion calls for joy, such as a marriage celebration. Feel sad when you lose someone you love. Feel fear when your life is threatened, as in an earthquake or natural disaster.

Natural, spontaneous feelings are always right in response to real things, real people, and real situations. We feel happy when we attain success; we feel sad when we fail to achieve our goal; we feel angry when someone abuses or exploits us; and we feel frightened when there is a life-threatening situation. They come spontaneously without conscious deliberation and direction. Never fake your feelings and pretend otherwise.

Express your feeling. Let it come and go like the cloud. Never repress it, and let it stay in yourself. Repressed anger, when accumulated more than we can tolerate, will explode in an uncontrollable and destructive rage with serious consequence.

There are two types of feelings. One is original, natural, unconditioned, and spontaneous feeling, and the other is acquired, unnatural, conditioned, and habitual feeling. Fear is a natural feeling, but phobia is an unnatural, conditioned feeling built into our self. Many people have built-in phobias of spiders, snakes, height, darkness, strangers, etc. Phobia is a permanent part of the personality and is difficult to get rid of.

Hatred, anger, worry, anxiety, grief, envy, and depression can be conditioned and entrenched in our personality. Racists are conditioned to hate other races, and they have a built-in hatred that is a permanent part of their personality. Acquired built-in ill feeling is bad for health, body, and soul. Natural feeling comes and goes, but acquired conditioned feeling stays forever in the system.

There is nothing wrong with our natural feelings. It is wrong to label them good or bad, right or wrong, or positive or negative. Natural feelings inform us of the real situation, including how we react and what we do can be—good or bad, right or wrong. When you are angry and you assault someone, your action is not right and is not good. Unnatural feelings that are conditioned, entrenched, and acquired through conditioning are bad, wrong, and negative. Conditioned ill feeling like conditioned reflex is acquired through conditioning or training.

Trust your natural feelings. They cannot be wrong. They inform us accurately of the real situation. Feelings cannot arise by themselves. They are aroused by something within us and something outside us.

Chapter 14

The Life of Freedom

*H*eaven has given humankind free will and the freedom to live their own lives. Free will is our most precious endowment or gift from God. Since every human is born with free will, he has the freedom of choice, the power to choose what he likes or dislikes. Liberty, or freedom of choice, is our divine right. If we cannot choose or select, then we are not free.

We must use our free will rightly and wisely to be the master of our own lives, to be our own true selves, to do what is good and right, and to be a master and not a slave to a religion, authority, government, or any man-made thing.

The vast majority of mankind is not free, because as a child, you are not the master of your own life. You are not independent but dependent on your parents. You live the life prescribed by your parents. You are told how to behave, what to do, and what religion, custom, or tradition to follow.

From childhood, you submit to your parents, teachers, priests, friends, relatives, and all kinds of people who have authority over you. You accept their thoughts, feelings, actions, behaviours, customs, traditions, and religions without question because you are under their control. You are subjected to training, brainwashing, indoctrinating, and programming to be a conformist person with the same conformist mentality and conduct.

You are not your true self as you are not in charge of your life. You have no original thoughts of your own because you are too young to reason and to originate your own thoughts. You follow blindly the beliefs, opinions, suggestions, theories, dogmas, doctrines, and all kinds of thoughts. You do not know whether they are true or false, right or wrong, good or bad, but you accept them without question. You grow up living the life prescribed by others.

As an adult, you are independent and you can exercise your free will to change your life for the better, not the life dictated by parents, priests, teachers, and others. However, it takes time to unlearn all the past errors, to deprogram the programs or thoughts in your mind, to de-condition the conditioning and bad habits, to change yourself for the better, and to be the master of your own life.

Freedom is a prerequisite in the perfect reproduction of love, beauty, happiness, peace, harmony, creativity, goodness, rightness, power, and life. Freedom is the most precious thing on Earth when you do not have it. Many people take freedom for granted. They never know that millions sacrificed their lives so that we can live a free life.

If God compels or forces us to accept or reject anything without choice or freedom, would there be any freedom in that kind of person? Such a person should be a mere robot with no sense of liberty at all. God forbids that any of us should become automatons or blind followers of any religion or custom. Since God has given us free will, the divine will leave us alone to think how to live our lives.

Freedom must be based on wisdom. We are free to do the right thing but never any wrongdoing. We are free to do good deeds but never any evil. We choose what is good, right, beautiful, just, peaceful, harmonious, joyful, noble, and divine. Freedom is the absence of total control, bad laws, and submission to man-made institution. Free will is the true nature of the mind, the absence of mindsets and programmes.

Chapter 15

The Life of Now

*N*ow is real. It is an ever present reality. The past exists only in memory, and the future is a dream. Every minute, every day, every year becomes a memory as soon as it has passed. Everything happens now. Not to act and achieve now is not to act and achieve at all. You can only think, feel, do, and live now, not in the past or in the future. Not to be so in the present is not to live at all.

Your future success begins now. Not to do anything now means there is no future. When you are thinking and living in the past or future, you are missing the present. You are forgetting to live now. If you want to get rid of your bad habits, do it now. Never say, "I will do it tomorrow or some other time." Never delay or postpone what you can do now. Procrastination achieves nothing. It is always a dream.

Say to yourself, "I will live my ideal life now. I will manifest my ideal life now." It is a good habit to do what needs to be done now or as soon as possible. Procrastination is a bad habit. It can never get things done. Your future success depends on what you do now or at the earliest opportunity.

Today is real, yesterday was gone forever, and tomorrow is yet to come. To think about the past is to relive the past, which is a complete waste of time. To think about the past, about lost opportunity and the good old days, makes you sad. To worry about the uncertain future makes you anxious and tearful. You can plan for the near future but not the distant future. Not to think about the past or the future gives you peace of mind and the joy of living a real life.

For God, there is neither past nor future, beginning nor end. There is only the eternal now, or eternity. This is God's time, absolute time, the eternal now, forever and ever. Heaven does everything now. You have an eternal soul that does things in the eternal now, not in the past or future.

Ancient Sanskrit poem

Look to this day
for it is life,
the very life of life.

In its brief course lie all
the realities and truths of existence:
the joy of growth,
the splendours of action,
the glory of power.

For yesterday is but a memory
And tomorrow is only a vision.

But today well lived
makes every yesterday a memory
of happiness
and every tomorrow a vision of hope.

Look well, therefore, to this day . . .

Chapter 16

Life of the Mind

We have only one mind, but there are two modes of mind, and each is working differently and has different functions. One is the material, objective, conscious mind; the other is the spiritual, subjective, subconscious mind. Everyone knows the working and functions of the objective mind, but very few know and understand the subjective mind.

It is the coordination of these two modes of mind, the right understanding of their functions that is the great secret of life. With this knowledge, we can bring the objective and subjective mind into close cooperation and working harmoniously with one another without conflict. A mind divided will split the personality and adversely affect the optimal functioning, well-being, and mental efficiency of the whole mind. Mental efficiency rests on harmony; discord means confusion.

The two modes of mind have two very important functions to sustain life. One is voluntary, willed, deliberative, conscious action; the other is involuntary, spontaneous, automatic, subconscious function.

The subconscious mind is concerned with spontaneous function of the heart, lungs, and other internal organs that sustain life. All these organs function spontaneously or automatically without any conscious direction. The subjective mind does not sleep. It works twenty-four hours a day throughout life. There is certainty and regularity without any possibility of error in the operation of the life process. Such vital function cannot be delegated to the objective mind that has to deliberate and will every action. Such function must be spontaneous or automatic.

The great lesson in life is to let most of our essential daily activities become habitual and automatic without conscious direction of the objective mind. Playing the piano, using the typewriter, and riding a bicycle require conscious direction and effort. At first, the process is slow, laborious, and erroneous. With constant practice and repetition, they become automatic. We just do them effortlessly. *Wu-wei,* or effortless action, is the way of the Tao. The Tao is spontaneous. 自然

The objective mind is concerned with all conscious action that can be directed and controlled at will. The external body is under the direction and control of the objective mind. We can walk, stop, and change direction at will; we can raise or lower our hands; we can move our heads up and down consciously. But we cannot stop our heartbeats, the circulation of the blood, the production of body cells, healing of the body, and many other internal life processes.

The objective mind goes to sleep every night and ceases all activities of the outer body. However, the inner vital organs do not stop functioning. They operate ceaselessly without a break. It is unthinkable that such vital functions are under the control of the objective mind that goes to sleep every night.

It is true that conditions of disease, fear, worry, poverty, disharmony, disorder, confusion, and evil of all kinds are the result of wrong thoughts, false beliefs, and erroneous suggestions being accepted by the unguarded, subjective mind that manifested them in life. The important duty of the objective mind is to act as watchman to prevent entry of false beliefs, perverse ideas, abnormal views, and wrong thoughts into the subjective mind. Sick thoughts make a sick mind; right thoughts make a right mind.

The objective mind thinks; the subjective mind feels. The objective mind thinks numerous kinds of thoughts, such as doctrines, dogmas, beliefs, opinions, suggestions, isms, ideologies, theories, facts, and truths. We are what we think. What kind of thoughts we put into the subjective mind and what we think from these thoughts make us what we are. Christian thoughts make a Christian, Buddhist thoughts make a Buddhist, racist thoughts make a racist, good thoughts make a good man.

To have a good mind and a right mind, we must be ever careful of the thoughts that gain entry into the subjective mind. Now it is true that when you think health, your body manifests health as it does peace. All right thinking originates in and is of God. Thought is the modus operandi of God. Divine mind is really right mind with right thinking.

Knowing the truth is really right thinking. When you are thinking right about a thing, you are knowing the truth about it. Know the truth, and the truth will set you free. Your mind is free from untruths, lies, and wrong thoughts. Your mind is liberated and enlightened. The right mind is the enlightened mind, the divine mind, and it knows the truth.

Chapter 17

The Life of Desires

Life or death? Desire or no desire? Desire is the very life of every living thing. Without desire, life could not exist. Desire is the power behind all living things, the moving principle of the universe, and the innermost centre of all life. To end desire is to end life. To manifest desire is to fulfil life.

Desire is the creating principle of creation, whether it is the universe or a boat; both have their origin in the desire to bring something into existence that does not exist. Whatever may be the scale on which we use our creating ability, the motive power must always be desire. It is absolutely true that desire is the cause of all thoughts, all actions, and all life. If devoid of desire, there is no motive to act or to live.

Where there is life, there are desires. We desire a good life, not just mere, existence. We desire comfort, peace, health, happiness, freedom, prosperity, security, harmony, love, beauty, and all the good things in life. Always desire what is good, right, noble, beautiful, true, and natural but never the bad, evil, ugly, perverse, and unnatural. Good desire is divine. It is the divine self seeking fuller expression of life. Trust your desire.

There is only one divine desire: to give life, love, peace, harmony, wisdom, freedom, and beauty to mankind. "I am come that you might have life and have it more abundantly." That was the life mission of Jesus. The desire for the advancement, betterment, improvement, and continuous progress of mankind is a godly one. The desire for power, authority, greed, control, and fame is ungodly. It is not good and not right.

The economy, cultures, civilizations, and all the creations in the world are products of our desires. The food industry—fisheries, farms, cafes, restaurants, shops, and supermarkets—are created to fulfil our hunger and desire for food. There are many kinds of food: fresh fruits and vegetables, frozen meat, process food, dry food, canned food and others. Food production employs millions of people worldwide.

The winery, bottling industry, coffee shops, and teahouses are there to satisfy our thirst and desire for drinks. There are many kinds of drinks: soft drinks, mineral water, fruit juice, beer, wine and alcohol to satisfy the different needs of the people.

The construction industry that builds hotels, motels, and millions of houses is built on our desires for shelter and accommodation.

All the books in the libraries, schools, universities, and other places of learning are there to satisfy our desire for learning, knowledge, and know-how.

The jumbo jet plane, super ocean cruisers, buses, trains, and millions of motorcars, as well as the tourism industry, are created to cater for our desire to travel.

The hospitals, dental clinics, drug industry, doctors, and nurses look after our desire for health.

The textile industry and the shoe factories make millions of articles of clothing and pairs of shoes to meet our desire to keep warm in winter and cool in summer.

Thank Heaven for the desires. If not, there would be no progress, no world trade, and no industry. Without human desires, the world economy would collapse and civilization would end. Truly, desire is the creating principle of the world, the mother of all creations. Everything is made, produced, manufactured, and created to fulfil our desires directly and indirectly.

Desire for the most beautiful, the most ideal, the greatest, the noblest, the highest, the best, the most valuable, and the truest is absolutely good. To know God, to seek enlightenment, should be the supreme desire of every educated man and woman. If you do not have the desire, there will be no fulfilment. Desire has fulfilment for its correlatives. Desire and fulfilment are bound together as cause and effect.

Chapter 18

The Life of Change

*I*Ching 易经, *Book of Changes,* is the ancient Chinese thought on change. Change is the fundamental principle and reality in the universe. It is permanent reality in the natural world and the man-made world. Change is real and is everywhere in the home, in the environment, in nature, and in the world. We see and experience changes every moment, every minute, every day. According to the I Ching, Heaven is the first cause behind all the changes in the universe. It is continuous forever and ever. It is inevitable, unavoidable, and inescapable.

Without change, there is no creation, no new things, no development, no improvement, no growth, no advancement, and no progress. Without change, nothing exists. Change can be slow or fast, gradual or sudden, peaceful or violent, predictable or unexpected. Slow, gradual changes are the norm; sudden, quick changes are the exception. The change in the seasons is slow and gradual. It is regular and predictable.

There are two ways to affect changes. One is the process of combining and adding; the other is the process of separating and subtracting. By combining sodium and chlorine, we create a new compound called sodium chloride or salt. Water can be separated into hydrogen and oxygen, two different elements. These two processes give rise to all the things in the world.

Life is a continuous process of change, growth, and development. The desire to change for the better is inherent in every human being. We desire a good life, a better life, and the best of life. We want more health, more happiness, more peace, more harmony, more prosperity, more love, and more good things in life. It is change for the better that brings us the things we desire.

To change your life for the better, you must first change your thoughts. You are the sum total of your thoughts. The same old thoughts make the same old you—never the new you. Only new thoughts can make a new you. First and foremost, have a right knowledge or understanding of your true nature, self, and life. Without the truths or right thoughts, you cannot have the right mind to think right, feel right, do right, and live right.

To begin with, do a thorough mental house cleaning to get rid of all the junk that has accumulated in your mind. Get rid of all your wrong thoughts, bad thoughts, evil thoughts, ugly thoughts, and useless thoughts, and replace them with thoughts that are right, good, beautiful, and useful.

Replace the old with the new, and the old thoughts will not dehumanize you anymore.

Change yourself for the better. Man is made and unmade by his thoughts. He is the maker of his character, the moulder of his life, and the builder of his destiny. A man is truly what he thinks; his character is the sum total of his thoughts. A good and upright character is not a thing of favour or chance but is the natural result of continuous effort in right thinking. Selfish and petty thoughts make a selfish and petty personality. As within, so without. The inner is manifested in the outer. Replace the petty false self with your giant true self.

To change the world for the better, we must change our thoughts or mindsets. The world today is the result of the same old mindsets that passed down from the previous generations to the present generation. Don't expect any changes in the world with the same mindsets. Change our mindsets, and the world changes for the better. Real change, the cause of change, is always internal. Inner thoughts are the cause; external conditions are the effect.

Progress is ever changing for the better. It is continuous improvement and betterment of life, things, conditions, and all man-made things. However desirable or perfect our world may be, we should continue to improve upon it constantly. When we cease to promote progression, we return to the ways of retrogression.

The only way to progress is to move forward and upward. Not to go forward is to move backward. Not to move up is to fall down. We have to continue to make progress. When we stop, rest, and enjoy, we tell ourselves that it is the best and need no betterment, we are stagnating and regressing. Real progress is continuous. To live the life of change for the better is to advance every moment.

Chapter 19

The Life of Thinking

"*I* think, therefore I am," Descartes said. You are what you think. The aphorism "As a man thinketh in his heart, so is he" not only embraces the whole of a man's life but is so comprehensive as to reach out to every condition of his life. A man is truly what he thinks, his character being the sum total of his thoughts.

A man's character is shaped by his thoughts; his feelings are generated by his thoughts; his actions are decided by his thoughts; his behaviours and conduct are the result of his thoughts; his future and destiny are generated by his thoughts; his conditions are the effects of his thoughts; his life is determined by his thoughts.

Our thoughts determine what we are and who we are. We are Christians, Muslims, Buddhists, Hindus, atheists, humanists, Darwinists, and whatever because of our corresponding thoughts. You cannot be a Christian with Buddhist thoughts or beliefs. You know you make your thoughts, but you never know your thoughts make you.

Impure thoughts within are manifested through obscene language and indecent behaviour without. You cannot be decent when you have a dirty mind with filthy thoughts. Thoughts of fears, doubt, and indecision are manifested through conditions of failure bondage and dependence. Beautiful thoughts are expressed through elegance of a person's character and the beauty of his appearance, home, and conditions. Whatever thoughts we have—good or bad, true or false, right or wrong, positive or negative—cannot fail to produce results in the character and conditions.

This is the most important fact or truth in life. Everything must have its origin in the mind as a thought or an image. The airplane jets, ocean cruisers, computers, roads, motorcars, cities, political systems, governments, religions, philosophies, arts, tools, weapons, cultures, civilizations, and all man-made things must first begin in the mind as thoughts or images. No such thought, no such thing.

Thought is a power in itself. It is a vital living force, the most vital and subtle power in the universe. Thought is one of the greatest forces or powers in the universe because it is a spiritual power. To make it useful and practically available, we must know the principles, cause, and way it works. Rightly used, it is a creative power; wrongly used, it is a destructive power.

Your thought is an attractive power. It attracts whatever is most dominant in the mind. Like attracts like. Your good thought will attract all the good things in life. Your evil thought will attract all the evils to you. Never underestimate the power of your thoughts. Never take your thoughts for granted. Have great awe and respect to the power of your thoughts.

Thought is a very powerful force in our lives. Thoughts can create or destroy, make or unmake, liberate or enslave, pacify or enrage, heal or kill, encourage or discourage, make us healthy or sick, happy or sad. Thought is such a powerful force that it is of utmost importance that we have only the right thoughts and the good thoughts in the mind.

Your mind is the most valuable asset; your quality of life depends on it. So take good care of it. Only good thoughts, right thoughts, noble thoughts, beautiful thoughts, creative thoughts, and healthy thoughts are welcome. Wrong thoughts, bad thoughts, evil thoughts, ugly thoughts, perverse thoughts, and sick thoughts are prohibited entry into the mind. If you have such thoughts in mind, get rid of them and replace them with good ones.

Every right thought, noble thought, and good thought that is put into the mind comes into life. Every wrong thought, bad thought, and evil thought that is taken out of mind is taken out of life.

Right thought makes a right mind; good thoughts make a good mind. With the right mind, you can think right, feel right, do right, and live right. Everything is right in your life. Wrong thought create wrong feeling, wrongdoing, and wrong living; wrong thoughts are causing all the problems in your life and in the world.

The life you are living right now is the result of everything you have thought all the way through life. All these thoughts determine the decisions you make, and the decisions you make determine your actions; the actions you make determine your position and future. Change your thoughts, and you change your decisions, which changes your actions, which changes your life.

Chapter 20

The Life of Health

erfect health is the first priority in life. It is necessary to do one's best in life, to live life to the fullest, to fully enjoy life, to get everything of worth from life that life has to give, and to fulfil the purpose of life and realize the fullest measure any aim, ambition, aspiration, or ideal one may have in view of life.

Perfect health is total well-being that includes mental well-being, emotional well-being, spiritual well-being, and physical health and fitness. They are all interconnected and interrelated. Mental illness will affect the overall health despite one having good physical health. Nowadays, more people are suffering from emotional sickness and mental sickness as well as physical sickness. Health is the absence of sickness and diseases.

Good health is the optimal functioning of all the organs in the body. Any malfunctioning in the heart or kidney will adversely affect the health of the body. Avoid smoking, as it causes damage to the lungs and causes cancer. Avoid drinking alcohol, as it causes severe damage to the liver.

Good health is the absence of all conditioned ill feelings, such as phobia, depression, anxiety, worry, anger, and hatred. The body should be in perfect equilibrium and peace. All these ill feelings have a harmful effect to the body.

A healthy body has a good immune system to fight diseases and recover quickly. It has the power of healing wounds and injury. It has a good circulatory system where blood flows freely without blockage or obstruction. It can get rid of all toxins and waste efficiently. It has a good digestive system to assimilate nutrients and to get rid of waste properly.

To have good health, we must fulfil our basic needs. What is essential to life is also essential to health. We need good food to maintain and build the body. We need water to purify the body by flushing out waste matter in the body. We need fresh air for the respiratory system, and we need sunlight to keep warm. There are also essential needs like clothes and shelter.

For good health, we must eat the right food. Eat more fresh fruits and vegetables and less meat. Avoid fatty and salty food to prevent high blood pressure and other degenerative sickness. Your body and your health result from what you eat. Eat junk food, and you have a sick body. Eating the wrong food causes many kinds of degenerative sickness, such as diabetes, arthritis, hypertension, and cancer.

Exercise regularly to improve health. Walking and jogging are the best forms of exercise. They are natural and effective. Everyone, from children to elderly people, can exercise. Walking and jogging can be practiced anywhere, anytime, but preferably in the park and in the morning. Running may be too strenuous for the elderly, but walking and jogging are good alternatives for them. Walking and jogging should be moderate and vigorous, lasting at least ten minutes to half an hour to have good results. Exercise improves health by adding stamina, strength, endurance, and fitness to the body.

A good night of sleep is essential to a healthy body. The body is revitalized every night during sleep. We must have sufficient sleep to stay healthy. Too little or insufficient sleep will destroy health and diminish the vitality of the body. Prevention is better than a cure and laughter is the best medicine. Nowadays, we can easily access information and knowledge on the Internet concerning health and well-being. Also, there are scores of books on health and well-being available in the library and in the bookshop.

Chapter 21

The Life of Light

There are two kinds of light: material light and spiritual or divine light. Sunlight, candlelight, and torchlight enable us to see material things with our eyes. Without light, there is total darkness and we can't see a thing.

Our eyes can see and differentiate things, colours, magnitude, height, space, distance, depth, size, quantity, quality, beauty, transparency, movement, stillness, darkness, and light. The eyes can see material light but not divine light. The latter is invisible.

Physical blindness is the incapacity to see material things; spiritual blindness is the inability to see God or Heaven. Heaven is divine light. This divine light is in every human being.

Enlightenment means to be illuminated or enlightened by divine light, to know one's true nature or self, to know God, to experience divine bliss, to be one with Heaven (Tian ren he yi) 天人合一, and to have a brilliant, unconditioned mind.

"All are parts of one stupendous whole whose body nature is, and God the soul"

Alexander Pope

"Our birth is but a sleep and a forgetting: The soul that rises with us, our life's star, . . . But trailing clouds of glory do we come From God, who is our home."

William Wordsworth